M000087377

100 SONNETS FOR OUR TIME

"Jeff's poetry portrays deep emotion through complex forms all while maintaining the warm intimacy of an old friend."

—GRAHAM MAURO, poet,
linguist, former student

"So strong and emotional....and beautiful; I'm grateful to you."

—MORLEY HEGSTROM, educator

"Just in time, and well-versed."

—LYNETTE WILLIAMS, educator

"Jeff Wyman's sonnets are a time capsule of experiences from a year like no other. They offer hope and perspective in a time of isolation and uncertainty."

—MADDIE BLUMM, educator,
actor, former student

"Thank you, Jeff, for your sonnets through the pandemic; I've come to look forward to them week by week as, I'm sure, have many others."

—ZACH STEWART, educator, writer

"These sonnets are about finding hope, purpose, and community in the most challenging time of our lives."

—LARRY LEWIN, educator, author

100 Sonnets for Our Time

JEFF WYMAN

LUMINARE PRESS
WWW.LUMINAREPRESS.COM

100 Sonnets for Our Time
Copyright © 2021 by Jeff Wyman

All rights reserved. This book or any portion thereof may not be reproduced
or used in any manner whatsoever without the express written permission of
the publisher, except for the use of brief quotations in a book review.

Printed in the United States of America

Photo by OC Gonzalez on Unsplash

Luminare Press
442 Charnelton St.
Eugene, OR 97401
www.luminarepress.com

LCCN: 2021916524
ISBN: 978-1-64388-801-9

Dedicated to all you poetry-lovers out there

Contents

Where Do I Go From Here?

Where do I go from here; what more to do
If per chance the aging muses still speak,
Be you so kind as to give me a clue,
What more in life should I better now seek
My life has been spent by serving you well,
And certainly that has treated me kind,
But legs grow weary and words lose their spell,
When one cannot reach the unwilling mind.
What if there is light ahead on the road,
Nothing completely extinguished the fire,
And beneath the flames an ember still glowed,
Warming the path when it's time to retire.
There are poems to write, songs I must sing,
Much more to know of and much love to bring

The Poet

———•———

Who shares the heart's tale if not the teller
And asks not in return but enjoyment
Who lives in the feelings but the dweller
And casts spells just for love or employment
Who would dare make a project of sorrow
While putting intimate thoughts on display
And from nature or dreams only borrow
Creating resonant lines to repay
With pen in hand she slays mighty dragons
Or comforts children with visions of peace
Traveling time on dust-covered wagons
Sheltering rhymes only meant for release
The harvest yields fruit to those who grow it
So ask the truth of only the poet

What Do I See

What do I see when I look at your face
What is revealed there that turns on the light
Aside from the beauty that one can't replace
There's so much more that makes everything right
Shining beneath that most lovely facade
Lies a sweet disposition unsparing
And also, which leaves me grateful and awed
There's intelligence, wisdom, and caring
But for sure I believe it's worth sharing
We're not talking of someone fainthearted
She is also fun-loving and daring
An idea will just make her get started
So looking at you just makes me think of
Someone to believe in, someone to love

My Cancer Tree

Today I sat beneath my cancer tree
   As I often did that difficult year
   When I wondered what the answer would be
Steady recovery or realized fear
Her branches told stories of survival
As they bowed and curtsied so gracefully
Through winter storms and springtime revival
She whispered her wisdom yet silently
I paid my respects through the wind and rain
And was overcome with humility
Then slowly but surely began to gain
A new emotional security
I recovered my health and energy
But not without help from my cancer tree.

My Shadow

I chanced to see my shadow yesterday
It reminded me of when I was four
I wonder if I've changed in any way
Am I still the same boy I was before
My shadow used to fill me with wonder
This version wasn't quite me but almost
And now that life has torn me asunder
This duality has kept me engrossed
Who then is this shadow that follows me
Or sometimes even walks slightly ahead
When identity crises swallow me
Should I assume by him I've been mislead
I believed my shadow when I was four
I'll trust in him now and try evermore

Let Her Go

If you really love her then let her go
Don't try to control so potent a force
If it's genuine you must let it show
By respecting her wish without remorse
You didn't know how badly you hurt her
Until that sad night she said we were through
You had thought you would never desert her
But now it seems it's the right thing to do
As time marches on perhaps she'll forgive
And allow you back into her orbit
But just remember it's her life to live
You must gather this truth and absorb it
Your mind may say this will make you feel blue
But your heart says it's the right thing to do

Corona Time

The world feels like it's coming to an end
Everyone is scared so many are sick
Although the president tries to pretend
His lies don't match what the experts predict
Streets are deserted the rain just won't quit
It looks like the zombie apocalypse
This is our worst so it's best to admit
That nothing else can begin to eclipse
But folks on my screen get me through the day
And help with the weight of isolation
And not having to work, although no pay
Is a very odd sort of vacation
The rain takes a rest, the room fills with light
Offering hope that we'll get past this blight

Corona Time 2

My eye itches but I don't dare scratch it
Going crazy always being inside
Avoiding outside so I don't catch it
Maybe I'll get in my car for a ride
So I hit the road just to feel alive
There will be no traffic so I can cruise
But I've almost forgotten how to drive
Guess I'll go back inside and watch the news
Took a walk with a friend the other day
Going in style with my gloves and my mask
But social distance at six feet away
Means conversation is no easy task
So I leave my friend but he understands
I must go home and start washing my hands

Spark

I'm waiting for that big spark once again
The one that brings excitement to my life
I long to be the person I was then
Who doesn't only see a world in strife
My head is consumed by a potpourri
Thoughts range from dread to confusion to hope
Is this land someplace we still want to be
Are we learning or just trying to cope
We're all living with great uncertainty
About this disease and all that it's caused
Can we overcome the adversity
Of a country whose functioning has paused
With racial injustice under attack
I'm beginning to feel that spark come back

Responsibility

Responsibility must sustain us
By helping each other in times of need
We must not let this crisis restrain us
From doing what we must do to succeed
The federal government has failed us
Leaving people so angry and confused
Their blatant misguidance has derailed us
Lies and false promises can't be excused
Many state officials are working hard
To help guide us in the right direction
But if we the people let down our guard
We won't be able to gain protection
So isolate wear masks and wash your hands
It's what responsibility demands

About Being Depressed

———————◆———————

I'm intolerant of being depressed
Everything in me seeks enlightenment
Though at times I can't help feeling distressed
I'm in constant fear that I might relent
I'm aware of the reasons we despair
And I have personal dragons to slay
To fault someone's sadness is most unfair
But for me I can't stand feeling that way
When bad thoughts enter my overworked mind
I try my hardest to push them away
Not giving up hope is one way to find
Possible answers to get through the day
I'm not sure if others feel as I do
But hanging in there can yield a breakthrough

Living Alone

Living alone during sheltering times
Is as challenging as people have said
Because writing songs and phrasing these rhymes
Can't stop all the chattering in my head
Without distraction from people nearby
My mind tends to wander obsessively
And even though I don't always know why
It disrupts my peace most aggressively
When you share your home with loved ones or friends
It can be stressful or hard to control
But with a hangup that just never ends
They can be there to advise or console
Don't take for granted those folks in your place
It's often better than a solo space

Regret

Regret is quite a useless emotion
It keeps you from existing in the now
And though compassion is your devotion
It's not going to change things anyhow
Even though you long for self-redemption
And feel guilty that you made a mistake
There may never really be exemption
So just move on and give yourself a break
Good people always want to do what's right
And have a hard time with self-forgiving
But dwelling on it morning noon and night
Is clearly not how you should be living
Regret is very natural I know
But learn your lesson and begin to grow

Be Creative

This moment is the best time to create
While we're sheltering with little to do
When school and work start it could be too late
Days without distraction are precious few
Play music build a table learn to cook
Draw and paint fix your car knit a sweater
Plant a garden start a blog write a book
Weave a basket make your sports skills better
It's not only important for your mind
It also really helps with your spirit
Because in hard times like these you will find
You may be stuck at home but not fear it
Who knows you could even write a sonnet
Mainly just create so get right on it

Nostalgia

We all look back on good times in our life
And remember feeling much more content
We always imagine there was less strife
So as we reflect we tend to lament
Nostalgia can be a mild depression
It implies that we were happier then
Longing for the past is a concession
To thinking we can't have that joy again
We fall into nostalgia quite often
Imagining those good days better spent
The lens we look through we tend to soften
I wonder how much we really invent
Let's concentrate on living in the now
And look back with more perspective somehow

Duet's 1ˢᵗ Birthday

As today marks a birthday for Duet
We all give heartfelt thanks and celebrate
One of the greatest joys to us as yet
Every year we'll feel happy on this date
Born from love raised with love and giving love
A most precious addition to the clan
The beautiful girl her parents dreamed of
Back when those dreams of parenthood began
Becoming much more aware every day
And you're beginning to crawl up a storm
You're certainly growing in every way
We watch in wonder seeing you transform
As earth completes its journey round the sun
Our beautiful child of the air turns one

First Serious Love

Thinking back on my first serious love
I don't mean a prior crush or romance
This was a union that just rose above
The more common trappings of circumstance
She was my lover my soulmate my friend
With music adventure and traveling
We were partners and seekers to the end
Even when the seams were unraveling
We parted ways and our lives took their course
Off to the dark and bright sides of the road
But she has remained a spiritual source
And our shared compassion has never slowed
Though decades have passed I'm still so aware
That my first real love was precious and rare

Saturday Matinee

I recall the Saturday matinee
Newsreels cartoons and a double feature
I would look forward all week to that day
Those movies were my dreams and my teacher
We three best friends all laughing on the bus
With our display of fleeting innocence
Excited about what awaited us
With twenty-five cents our only expense
I was transported to faraway lands
Rode the range with Indians and cowboys.
Shivered in the trenches with dirty hands
On stage with rockers making joyous noise
Now reflecting on my life I can say
Nothing topped the Saturday matinee

Easier

It's easier to be sad than happy
In a world where sadness seems to prevail
There's always so much that just feels crappy
It's so hard when our best intentions fail
There are of course many moments of joy
And maybe even off and on for weeks
We should reflect on these times and employ
A way to discover some new techniques
Work in a garden or take a long walk
Go online and find a game to download
Call up a friend and have a heartfelt talk
You may well find the bright side of the road
The bottom line of everything above
Appreciate the things that we can love

Be Careful

Be careful out there don't get complacent
You could still be exposed not knowing it
An innocent person who's adjacent
Might be infected without showing it
We're all going crazy staying inside
And chomping at the bit to go do things
When it comes to guidelines we must abide
And see what scientific research brings
I'm pretty shocked at some folks' behavior
Defying the rules of social distance
Do they really think Trump is our savior
With his self-serving talk of resistance
Trust your instincts and let wise heads prevail
If we're not cautious this whole plan will fail

American Racism

We are now facing a grave urgency
Quite aside from the scary pandemic
Of black people's state of emergency
Police brutality is endemic
George Floyd's killing is not isolated
It's all part of the original sin
Of black people being subjugated
The time for all to speak out should begin
The solution has to start at the top
From the president down to all guilty
And ingrained in each citizen and cop
We must remove anyone who won't see
Let the ashes of racism scatter
Stoking the fires that black lives matter

John's Wisdom

ohn Lennon once said love is all you need
A simple positive message of peace
I liked the premise but I disagreed
Can't be enough for suffering to cease
I was often a skeptical realist
But gradually began to change my mind
I thought John was being an idealist
But it depends on how love is defined
I think he meant empathy and giving
And these days we need that to just survive
If we're to find a new way of living
We must reach out and help each other thrive
Many good people bring love day and night
Let's take their lead and show that John was right

My First Rock 'n' Roll

*'ll never forget my first rock 'n' roll
  Listening to the radio one day
  Something hot ignited deep in my soul
And I was totally carried away
A man was singing "rock around the clock"
With a guitar solo that blew my mind
I was in some kind of ecstatic shock
All my other music was left behind
Bill Haley and the Comets were my start
Elvis Fats Little Richard Roy and Chuck
A raw and exciting new form of art
That changed the world and left us all awestruck
When I consider my life as a whole
It was thoroughly shaped by rock 'n' roll

Why I Love Sonnets

S onnets are my favorite poetic style
   There are several reasons this is true
    While many other forms will make me smile
Writing sonnets is what I love to do
There are fourteen lines ten syllables each
With a definite rhyme and rhythm scheme
It keeps your thoughts from getting out of reach
While you can succinctly
express your theme
People think sonnets have to be profound
That certainly applies to quite a few
But all I have to do is look around
And I can write one about something new
Though writing sonnets often can be hard
Someday I'll have as many as the Bard

Time For Change

These are potentially historic times
Even though things look really bad right now
Let's remove those who are committing crimes
Policies we must no longer allow
The police departments need to reform
Where racism is institutional
Some are aware of the gathering storm
And are acting more constitutional
Hundreds of thousands are out in the street
To protest a system that is corrupt
Trump and his enablers feel the heat
Their quest for power we will interrupt
The ones at the top we need to combat
In November vote for the Democrat

DACA

Deferred Action for Childhood Arrivals
Allows the Dreamers to stay here for now
One of their most important survivals
But staying here for good we must allow
The Supreme Court narrowly did its part
Blocking dirty deeds by the president
Now it's time for Congress to show some heart
Make each one a permanent resident
The Dreamers are our sisters and brothers
Many do the essential frontline work
We must tell Mitch McConnell and others
This important duty they cannot shirk
DACA is a national improvement
Let's make it part of the current movement

Young Friends

I'm oh so grateful to have my young friends
They give my life joy and meaning I need
By helping me as my outlook transcends
Notions that now must evolve and proceed
I've known these great folks for several years now
Since middle school days or sometimes before
We still stay in touch as time will allow
I follow their dreams and watch them explore
I once was the teacher and now I learn
About our modern world from these fine minds
And new ways of thinking I can discern
Broader perspectives of all different kinds
The more I can see how they grow and give
The more I enjoy a good way to live

Red Roses

I have three dozen red roses today
  With grace and beauty they help me get by
  They are a sweet life-affirming bouquet
A treat for my spirit and for my eye
These lovely species will bloom every spring
They give me great hope and security
And when I think of the love they can bring
I accept this world of impurity
I have my music and poems inside
So many feelings I now can convey
My roses helped reestablish my pride
When life's circumstances took it away
These are not flowers that grow by the vine
They are the folks who are dear friends of mine

Perfect Storm

I retired from the field that I love
After going through a year of cancer
And it feels really hard to rise above
Too many questions without an answer
Someone special who loved me withdrew it
Exacerbating newfound loneliness
I still feel so guilty that I blew it
When I will move on I can only guess
Then came the virus with isolation
Where old age put me in a high risk group
Days spent in quiet anticipation
Wondering when I'll be back in the loop
At this moment I'm clinging to the mast
I'll set sail again when the storm has passed

The Ship

The ship of America is sinking
So now it's a matter of who can swim
If you can't it's time for some rethinking
Otherwise your chances are pretty slim
We need to help folks learn to stay afloat
And teach them new ways to keep hope alive
Because it's futile to stay in the boat
Find that new horizon so we can thrive
If we can guide our friends to navigate
The muddy waters of bureaucracy
Perhaps then we can help anticipate
Slowing the currents of hypocrisy
Be generous kind and encouraging
And watch for the lifeboat for rescuing

My Aunt Claire

emories of Claire are with me today
Beloved younger sister of my mother
My respect and love are hard to convey
But these thoughts we can share with each other
A force of nature with a gentle heart
A brilliant mind and a very quick wit
An amazing person right from the start
No matter the challenge she'd never quit
She raised three great kids and some dogs as well
And each one's name would begin with a C
Smart and creative with great tales to tell
They're quite a remarkable family
My Aunt Claire has lived a very long time
And I would say it was a life sublime

Imagine the World

Imagine the world you want to live in
Long after the pandemic has ended
Let's fight for a new one and not give in
Until the broken parts have been mended
Now that we're chained by abnormality
And not in a position to break free
Let's visualize a new reality
And use this time to make each other see
We need a massive re-education
On how to keep the people safe and whole
Imagine global participation
With health and welfare as the common goal
Our modern world is truly very strange
So everyone imagine what can change

For Larry

A birthday wish for my buddy Larry
Through good times and bad he's always
been there
A true bonding I will always carry
And with whom I'm always eager to share
I've known Larry for seventeen years now
With music politics teaching and sports
We never run out of ideas somehow
We see things the same and are true cohorts
A distinguished career to be proud of
With fierce commitment to kids and teachers
And showing his grandkids all kinds of love
He has so many outstanding features
As I wish a happy day to my friend
I rejoice in a union that won't end

Portland

———◆———

This I think is my first angry sonnet
But the forces of fascism have to go
People of Portland are getting on it
Standing up to Trump's tyrannical show
Secret military police swooped down
On folks protesting racial injustice
Violently wreaking havoc on this town
And then Trump has the gall to say "trust us"
Although he claims to have a legal right
This is not part of our democracy
That's why we must always keep up the fight
To combat this wave of autocracy
We have to stop this sooner than later
And curtail this wannabe dictator

Love: The Longest Running Play

---

*L*ove is the playwright's strongest emotion
Sustaining us when the stage appears bare
Giving the actors hope and devotion
Gratification as scenes become rare
I've experienced love in many ways
Grand settings with diverse relationships
From a cast of players of bygone days
To fresh young faces with salvation scripts
Many an act with long intermissions
I as director unsure of the pace
Carefully blocking for new positions
To stay cohesive with adequate space
And when the curtain falls what shines from above
Is a bright ghost light and that would be love

Compartmentalizing

Today I took a walk among the trees
And their majestic beauty spoke to me
While stressing over Trump's troops and disease
An important thought re-awoke in me
Although what we thought we knew has shifted
And we are beset with many a woe
It's a matter of staying uplifted
Because there is still a long way to go
The trees reminded me to not forget
There's so much we still can appreciate
Since so many folks cannot do this yet
It's a privilege we should not abdicate
Though we must keep involved I realize
It's important to compartmentalize

I Used You

I used you for your ideas and insight
Exploited your need for my gentle role
Manipulated your constant delight
And pressured you with caring as my goal
I used you for someone I could support
And then maneuvered to be there for you
When you were depressed I schemed to consort
And offer comfort cuz I'd been there too
I used you for my grand inspiration
And subjected you to poem and song
Selfishly sharing my new creation
Knowing that making you happy was wrong
These are some evils that I have thought of
But the worst thing was I used you for love

Gratitude

Gratitude takes discipline I've been told
It's hard to not take good things for granted
First we must recognize what we behold
A new seed can't sprout till it's planted
Although normal life has come to a halt
Despair and nostalgia can't be my fate
And though our country is under assault
I'm glad I live in a beautiful state
Rather than dwell on someone who hurt me
And feel unhappy because I've been burned
I want my higher self to convert me
To recognizing the lessons I learned
Though it may take a shift in attitude
I'll work on always having gratitude

Cancel Culture

The cancel culture is unfortunate
If something offends you don't close the door
Yes, react but know how to portion it
The chances are you've made mistakes before
We on the left have to stick together
Because these days we have a common foe
Can't you see we are birds of a feather
If you can't forgive how can someone grow
If one refuses to apologize
For an offensive statement or action
Then you have every right to ostracize
But allow them to make a retraction
If canceling someone is your first move
I must question what you're trying to prove

Out of My Head

I wish I could get you out of my head
I'd surely be a much more peaceful man
To concentrate on something else instead
Would be helpful but I don't think I can
When I awake in the morning you're there
And you stay on my mind throughout the day
I just don't understand why I still care
Or continue to obsess in this way
One would think by now I could extricate
Myself from useless preoccupation
But my thoughts continue to replicate
I'm longing for a mental vacation
Someday you will be a fond memory
And I can choose my time of reverie

Normalization

Why is it normal to carry a gun
Or physically harm another being
This is to the benefit of no one
Are we looking without really seeing
Why is our president so outrageous
He breaks the law and continues to lie
Has accepting this become contagious
There should be a unanimous outcry
Is it normal in such a wealthy land
That more than half a million have no home
And yet government will not lend a hand
Is this just another common syndrome
These are but a few plaguing our nation
Let's not accept this normalization

My Muse

She was is and always will be my muse
Sparking a creative streak forever
So much inspiration she would infuse
A new and lifelong healing endeavor
I've never known someone so beautiful
Whose essence I would completely embrace
Productivity became dutiful
Just channeling that magnificent face
First my poems and songs were about her
Then they began to embrace different themes
And even at times when I might doubt her
She's always right there in my thoughts and dreams
Throughout my whole life I could never choose
A more compelling lovely perfect muse

2021

Here is my hope for 2021
Since this year has been a real disaster
Visions of a new life will have begun
And we'll move toward restructuring faster
The presidency we will rearrange
Only then can the healing get started
We'll get serious about climate change
And our commitment will be wholehearted
We'll have a real plan for the pandemic
See jobs returning and kids back in school
And Black Lives Matter will be endemic
With racial justice the practice and the rule
Clearly there is so much work to be done
But I have hope for 2021

A Battle Raging

There's a battle raging we can't ignore
It's the people versus Donald J Trump
It's gotten so we can't take any more
As the country goes deeper in this slump
He's destroying everything we hold dear
From democracy to morality
Dividing our land with hatred and fear
With corruption the new reality
With thousands dying he turns a blind eye
Denying science and telling us lies
Caring just for himself and so thereby
Leading our country to certain demise
Before this man has us all by the throat
The best way to win is to vote vote vote

Farewell RBG

W e're mourning the passing of RBG
One of the greatest people of all time
Our country has needed her desperately
With her spirit and intellect sublime
Unparalleled champion of human rights
And master of democratic dissent
Tirelessly winning many good fights
An amazing life so honorably spent
Her death leaves us frightened for what's to come
Can SCOTUS possibly do right by her?
A court representing all not just some
Or will it totally lose sight of her
Whatever happens we will remember
The loss of a hero this September

Hope

We can't mentally survive without hope
Though not denying what's happening now
Being optimistic can help us cope
And make life more enjoyable somehow
Hope can keep us positive in sad times
When little seems to be going as planned
It gives us incentive during bad times
To be more energized and take a stand
Thus having hope can spur us to action
And keep us focused on getting things right
In this sense it is not an abstraction
At the tunnel's end we can see a light
Hope springs eternal the poet would say
It seems essential for finding our way

The Flower

I held in hand a beautiful flower
By far the loveliest in the garden
It grew more alluring by the hour
Beckoning me for my grip to harden
Defying what the best artist could draw
With petals of a rare magnificence
I found myself in unparalleled awe
With feelings of major significance
I squeezed it too hard and the flower broke
And blew away in the cold winter wind
Though apologies were words that I spoke
I wish my act I could somehow rescind
I've gone to the garden many a time
But never beheld an herb so sublime

The Election

————•—•—————

We are now holding our collective breath
As this contentious election draws near
Hoping to avoid democracy's death
And taking action to overcome fear
It's the worst time in modern history
For corruption and voter suppression
It's clearly no longer a mystery
For the reasons behind this oppression
The president doesn't even pretend
To follow the rules like all those before
He won't leave when his term comes to an end
We need a blue wave to show him the door
If you're scared to see our best values go
Let's get out the vote and all vote for Joe

Your Face

I will never get tired of your face
I've cherished it over many a year
A door to the world a joy to embrace
My muse to create my star to revere
How to describe unparalleled beauty
While I contemplate it day after day
As a poet I guess it's my duty
To somehow attempt the words to convey
So rich and full with movement and grace
Like a grand sunrise and sunset combined
Great jewels from the East or Europe's fine lace
Radiance magnified richness defined
There is nothing on earth that could take the place
Of your glorious incomparable face

Pablo

ere's to the greatest poet of Chile
And one of the finest the world has known
My love and respect I want to relay
Through the years my admiration has grown
With sensual eloquence and much pride
He was uniquely able to convey
The ravishing beauty of his sweet bride
Who thrilled him by night and loved him by day
He wrote as he lived and lived as he wrote
The eternal quest for humanity
Penning great verses that millions would quote
While fighting against the insanity
The world won't forget such passion sublime
Pablo Neruda a voice for all time

Drop It Off

If you haven't mailed it in drop it off
You have until 8 PM on Tuesday
Please tell your apathetic friends who scoff
There could be a terrible price to pay
The most crucial election we have faced
Is here and we have to participate
If Trump wins our country will be disgraced
I beg you to vote before it's too late
People are waiting hours on long lines
Defying attempts to curtail their rights
If we join them to stop the evil signs
Democracy could still be in our sights
Oh please make sure your ballot is received
So that a better life can be perceived

Celebration

The US will have a real president
Rather than an incompetent phony
So now can the new White House resident
Heal a nation filled with acrimony
Even though the country is divided
It is still a time for celebration
Hopefully Donald Trump has provided
The past four years as an aberration
So much healing and good work to be done
Though I know we have a long way to go
The world could be better for everyone
If we all support Kamala and Joe
Americans are stressed out and tired
But relieved and happy that Trump was fired

What She Gave

———————•———————

Her loveliness was truly a treasure
One that I was so fortunate to find
Bestowing unprecedented pleasure
From multitudes of attributes combined
With men she didn't have to compromise
Though she struggled with insecurity
But with our friendship there was no disguise
Just a sense of natural purity
With her loving face she'd listen to me
Making me feel valued and respected
And those caring eyes would glisten for me
As we became powerfully connected
Although our ties we needed to sever
I will cherish and love her forever

Return To Trust

Under Trump we've seen a huge loss of trust
Even doubting reliable sources
But trusting hard evidence is a must
Pay heed to what an expert endorses
The norm has been that lying is okay
Making it hard to know what to believe
The president does it to get his way
Not caring that people will misconceive
It's imperative to change this thinking
By renewing faith in science and facts
If not our chances will keep on shrinking
For fighting Covid with effective acts
Wear a mask social distance don't complain
Without having trust there's little to gain

I Never Meant To
Fall In Love

———— • ————

I never meant to fall in love with you
  Or have you become a new obsession
  You know that's not what I set out to do
To ever give you the wrong impression
I adored who you were as a person
And that brought almost enough excitement
But then my weakness began to worsen
As you turned on the charm and enticement
Your allure and beauty were riveting
And the combination was just too much
I slowly found my feelings pivoting
From friendship to desiring your touch
I never meant to fall in love with you
But stopping I was not able to do

Thankful

oday as we celebrate Thanksgiving
I am truly grateful for all I've been shown
To all the folks who make life worth living
And to privilege I've been blessed to have known
So many people are hurting right now
And my heart breaks for their struggle and pain
As this government deserts them somehow
I'm thankful this president won't remain
I'm thankful for my family and friends
And the joy they've brought me over the years
From all the love that simply never ends
And how they've helped with my dark times and fears
So as I sit here being reflective
I'm most thankful for my clear perspective

The Gallery of Dreams

I gaze upon the gallery of dreams
My fantasies real yet idealistic
Dominating my mind or so it seems
Complex but at the same time simplistic
The stirring movement of eyes and lips
Erasing my peripheral vision
From boyhood to manhood circular trips
A continuing timeline collision
Unbridled sensuality unleashed
Am I purposely being transported
Epitome of madness nearly reached
Life as I've imagined it distorted
Surrendering to fancy in extremes
I gaze upon my gallery of dreams

Teachers

This is a tribute to teachers we know
On the front lines of civilization
Helping the kids and society grow
Working hard in a selfless vocation
They used to be honored trusted and praised
Guiding our children through learning and life
If you saw what they do you'd be amazed
Enduring long hours low pay and strife
Too often maligned unheard and controlled
Blame put upon them for others' mistakes
Unfair assertions the public's been sold
Let's change the narrative do what it takes
Multiple heroes appear in our ranks
That includes teachers so please give them thanks

Happy New Year

———•———

It's a new year and somehow we survived
Battered bruised and confused but still standing
Looking ahead for our old life revived
There has not been a year more demanding
The vaccine is coming bringing us hope
That we will gain control of this
virus
And though it remains a slippery slope
At no time have we been more desirous
We avoided a near catastrophe
By electing a president who cares
Unlike the last years of rapacity
Our better morals and values he shares
Although there's much more that I could think of
I'll say Happy New Year sending you love

All That You Do For Me

---·—•—·---

If I want to go to my happy place
And forget all my troubles for a while
All I have to do is look at your face
And my worried frown will become a smile
If I'm in the mood to truly rejoice
And let fine melodies enrapture me
All I have to do is hear your sweet voice
And it's beautiful tone will capture me
If I should want inspiration to write
I merely conjure up thoughts of my muse
Then with great contemplation and insight
I instinctively know which words to choose
All that you do for me I can't believe
In ways I couldn't possibly conceive

The Definition of Beauty

---◆---

I checked the dictionary just in case
I wasn't sure how beauty is defined
On the page was a picture of your face
With all its glorious features combined
I thought wait a minute let's look online
So I googled the word's definition
There again was your face looking so fine
Another breathtaking exhibition
I then looked up synonyms just for fun
And what do you think each one presented
OK I exclaimed I guess I am done
And curtailed my search very contented
Without any doubt it's certainly true
All sources confirmed that beauty is you

Soft Love Hard Love, Part 1

I'll never forget the days of soft love
And how it made me feel so excited
Answering all that I'd ever dreamed of
With the promise that we'd stay united
I was happier than ever before
In a state of genuine elation
I could not possibly have asked for more
So much deeper than infatuation
But when it ended soft love turned to hard
Because feelings that strong don't disappear
It's true her withdrawal has left me scarred
But to renounce love would be insincere
So as soft love ends the hard love begins
But as you've heard before - love always wins

Soft Love Hard Love, Part 2

So how does one turn a soft love to hard
    To care for one who won't reciprocate
    When you run the risk that they will discard
Any attempt on your part to relate
When each time you're either met with reproach
Or worse yet no response whatsoever
On their feelings you don't want to encroach
So you question your very endeavor
However, I feel you should still believe
If it truly was love then it's enduring
And though it might not be what you conceive
Possibilities are reassuring
Though losing soft love can catch you off guard
Keep your love flowing even though it's hard

Failed Coup

We have just witnessed an attempted coup
Probably for the first time in our land
Initially no one knew what to do
Finally the police got it in hand
Imagine if the rioters were black
Just how swift the reaction would have been
We really need to get our country
back
From the perpetrators of lies and sin
But Georgia did give us some very good news
The end of Mitch McConnell's awful reign
Regardless of your political views
You have to embrace an end to the pain
It's now time for our country to rebound
And use this failed coup to turn things around

Lady Democracy

Democracy – our lady in waiting
Serving the people's court of intention
But victims of "The Lie" are negating
Her efforts to provide comprehension
Inflamed and incited by demagogues
These folks want to overthrow our lady
Spreading the word through their postings and blogs
They've rallied their troops through means most shady
But our lady is resilient and strong
Because of our love and dedication
And by knowing the insurgents are wrong
We have the resolve to save our nation
Though vulnerable and sometimes frail
Our Lady Democracy will prevail

January 20 - A Long Time Comin'

*T*hat winter day was truly momentous
And it sure feels like a long time comin'
With exceptions, there's been a consensus
To help Joe Biden hit the ground runnin'
We've suffered much over the past four years
With sickness loss and trepidation
But if we can somehow get past our fears
We could see hope return to our nation
Good change has already been enacted
Overturning destructive policy
And people have already reacted
Embracing the movement toward equity
There's much negativity to release
Let's proceed with optimism and peace

Perspective

*C*onflicts with people are often quite hard
And we sometimes aren't sure how to deal
We tend to put up a defensive guard
And that determines how we think we feel
Often it's a matter of perspective
In other words how do we perceive it
If we empathize and be reflective
We might find a new way to conceive it
You might feel disillusioned or betrayed
Then in a moment of lucidity
When you realize the role that you played
You may find that they had validity
If resolution is your objective
It couldn't hurt to change your perspective

Alliterative Alleviation

Structuring sonnets has made me more sane
Posting poems has provided much joy
Lingering over lines let me remain
Content to create a craft to employ
Pandemics present pure isolation
Can I conceivably stay connected
Deter detachment for the duration
So networking needs are not neglected
Conveying thoughts is thorough therapy
It's calming creative contemplation
Challenging with continued clarity
As quatrains quietly quell vexation
Pondering poems procure my motif
And surely sharing them shows me relief

Sadness

I really wish I could shake this sadness
And maintain my positive attitude
I know we live in a time of madness
But that is sounding like a platitude
I feel sorry for people in the world
Admittedly it's also for myself
Though I don't want my angst to be unfurled
I can't keep my emotions on a shelf
The blues sweep across me like a windstorm
And make me despair about tomorrow
Compared to many I am safe and warm
But that doesn't always ease my sorrow
The pandemic will end so I am told
And then this sadness should loosen its hold

The Dancer

———•———

As she moves with grace and agility
The audience is joyful and spellbound
With dedication and ability
Seamlessly gliding as she twirls around
With a commitment to command the stage
By a strongly concentrated mindset
Beginning from a very early age
She's trained her body for rigor and sweat
It's art it's sport it's choreography
With music an essential component
It's a form of movement biography
Great preparation now in the moment
If you're seeking a spirit enhancer
Go and behold the fabulous dancer

Embracing Not Knowing

We live in a world of information
Some of it factual some of it not
Being unsure causes trepidation
Keeping up with it all feels like a lot
How do we know which guidelines to follow
In order to feel most safe and secure
Which ones are solid which ones are hollow
This knowledge we think we need to procure
We drive ourselves crazy wanting to know
And that undermines results that we seek
It might be better to go with the flow
Employ a new preservation technique
Though we do need info to keep going
I think I'll try embracing not knowing

Conversation

*A*ll I need is a good conversation
With someone who's intelligent and kind
I'm not looking for a big sensation
Just an outlet to learn and speak my mind
Perhaps one pandemic silver lining
Is that we've had to reach out virtually
And to keep social skills from declining
Communication is shared mutually
With pearls of wisdom from many a friend
My mind and heart have greatly expanded
And when our sheltering comes to an end
We'll reopen this gift we've been handed
Quite essential to my preservation
Is counting on a good conversation

The Smell of Spring

I walked today in the Oregon spring
Inhaling the fresh smell of the season
As I tried to be one with everything
Without needing a rhyme or a reason
I thought of Georgia and the new Jim Crowe
And how Americans still love their guns
But then I saw the dogwood leaves aglow
And watched how the Willamette River runs
In this world it's easy to be distressed
But mother nature asks you to embed
With a young robin peering from its nest
And the blue sky sparkling overhead
We won't forsake the changes we must bring
Yet still rejoice in that sweet smell of spring

Lake at Four

This is for a wonderful boy named Lake
Who's smart talented and so very sweet
This is quite a rare child make no mistake
And being his grandpa is such a treat
He constantly has an interesting thought
And expresses ideas so very well
He picks up on whatever he's been taught
And it's a marvel to watch him excel
Music is already a huge passion
He plays piano drums and loves to sing
He pursues this in an intense fashion
We can picture the success this will bring
On his birthday from my heart I will pour
This is our amazing Lake at age four

The Cycle

You are happy today sad tomorrow
Monday full of hope but Tuesday despair
Joyful one day and the next day sorrow
For now optimistic then you won't care
Today you feel quite confident and strong
Tomorrow rather insecure and weak
Right now you're thinking you can do no wrong
But then you become self-conscious and meek
These are inherent cycles we go through
It's wise to accept the fluctuation
There is no lesson they mean to show you
Because it is not an aberration
This I'm afraid is the natural way
Take comfort from that and greet the new day

Seeker Survivor

I am a seeker and a survivor
Pursuing the flame avoiding the fire
A departee and constant arriver
Keeping my footing while climbing higher
I've enjoyed my share of recreation
And most certainly have followed a whim
But always believed in moderation
Fill up your cup but not to the brim
Looked for what's true and followed my hunches
Did not shy away from challenge I'd meet
Confronted wrong but rolled with the punches
Fighting to win but accepting defeat
All my life has been seek and ye shall find
But always survive for true peace of mind

Triggered

I'm triggered when I pass our favorite restaurant
  And I think of the great meals we had there
  Intense reflections continue to haunt
I don't want to go in and be sad there
I'm triggered when I see our coffee spot
Recalling conversations we enjoyed
Though I want to forget I just should not
Profound feelings aren't ones to avoid
I'm triggered when reminded of your voice
And all the sweet things that you'd say to me
But how I perceive that is my own choice
And regretful is not the way to be
I knew I'd struggle but never figured
That so many things would make me triggered

Visual Learner

I've realized I am a visual learner
I have learned so much from looking at you
And being an observant discerner
I could see all that great knowledge come through
Your strong body taught me orology
Where mighty peaks and crevasses divide
From your sweet lips I learned geography
How the oceans swell with the rising tide
Exotic eyes showed me geometry
And the variety of shapes and lines
The rest of your face taught astronomy
How the stars come out and why the sun shines
I now think I understand history
Still your beauty remains a mystery

Gentle People

Here's to all the gentle people out there
Who aren't racist and don't carry guns
Who help others and genuinely care
Knowing the rights they have are everyone's
If you watch the news we're in a bad state
With the angry rhetoric and violence
But folks I know are not consumed with hate
Yet do not want to resort to silence
Gentle people still want to speak their mind
And try to make our world a better place
There's a way to do this and still be kind
Without having to get in someone's face
We need peace both physical and mental
I rely on people who are gentle

First Move

The cop who killed George Floyd was convicted
Providing a much needed ray of light
Finally justice was not restricted
To those people who are privileged and white
Let's be clear this is just a beginning
There's a long way to go to reach a norm
And we really can't say we are winning
Until we have total police reform
Many calls don't need a badge or a gun
And police training has to be re-thought
Systemic racism must be undone
A nonstop battle that has to be fought
We all know there is so much to improve
But this conviction was a good first move

Beating The Bard

When it comes to sonnets there's just one king
And that of course would be William Shakespeare
But as you have seen they've become my thing
And I can write them too it would appear
He wrote 154 of them
A variety of topics quite deep
And every one was an absolute gem
He could write a masterpiece in his sleep
My sonnets are a bit more specific
And tend to be more conversational
But I seem to be just as prolific
Even though they are situational
And though I thought it would be much too hard
I've now written even more than The Bard

I Gather My Roses

I gather my roses in a bouquet
And marvel at their delightful essence
Providing what I rely on today
Inspired by their sweet effervescence
Throughout the season I enlist their charm
To fill me with great positivity
I'm protected from emotional harm
Restoring my hopeful proclivity
With lustrous sepals and fragrant petals
Offering genuine friendship and love
I feel a stillness as my mind settles
On the very things I'm most in need of
No matter the challenges life poses
I'll always have my bouquet of roses

One Kind Word

Just one kind word and you would set me free
From the guilt and self doubt I've been holding
A simple forgiveness would let me see
A new path to happiness unfolding
Merely one knowing smile would unlock me
From the tight bonds that keep my spirit chained
Loss and regret continue to block me
From furthering the insights I have gained
Only but one reconciling gesture
Would do much to change my sorrowful ways
Show you can shed your protective vesture
And I'll be grateful for all of my days
It would be so healing if I just heard
The sincere offering of one kind word

She Was

She was the precious girl who stirred my heart
But then became the woman who broke it
I truly adored her right from the start
Caring deeply though I never spoke it
Years went by and our relationship grew
With meaningful unmitigated joy
It was something quite special we both knew
Wisdom and youth an unlikely alloy
With all she gave I could not get enough
I somehow needed to invest in her
And losing her was incredibly tough
But I will always want the best for her
Yes, she was a girl who captured my heart
She'll stay there forever though we're apart

Divided

Will this country always be divided
Are we destined to forever distrust
Reason to agree has been provided
But common ground is not even discussed
Crass political manipulating
By those who seek money and power
Has fooled so many into conflating
Logic with the big lie of the hour
It's gotten to the point where out of spite
We think we're acting based on principle
We feel the need to argue and to fight
When our certainty is equivocal
If we remain a divided nation
We'll just spin our wheels for the duration

Get the Shot

*E*veryone must step up and get the shot
Overcome conspiracies and your fears
There are consequences if you will not
So many more illnesses deaths and tears
This problem of vaccine uncertainty
Seems that it really suggests denial
But the truth is there is an urgency
To stop this disease from going viral (pun intended)
We likely won't get herd immunity
Even if most people get the vaccine
But it's still best for our community
To protect from variants yet unseen
If you truly care or even if not
Now's the time to buck up and get the shot

The Gift That Keeps
On Giving

Teaching is the gift that keeps on giving
Both to the student and to the teacher
It has shown me a new way of living
With connections the outstanding feature
In the classroom I could always enjoy
Seeing so many students grow and learn
While relating to every girl and boy
With their appreciation in return
So now that I'm retired I have found
The fruits of my labor are evident
And simply what goes around comes around
Making my life's enrichment inherent
Teaching has been my greatest endeavor
A gift that I will cherish forever

My Mom

Today I will pay tribute to my mom
Without whom I would not be who I am
In a turbulent world she remained calm
When high water threatened she was my dam
With grace and sweetness she gave the world love
As she modeled goodness peace and respect
In a sky filled with hawks she was a dove
With kindness that had pervasive effect
Any good quality I may possess
I'd say it was mostly because of her
And if indeed I have had some success
It's to her wisdom that I shall defer
She left us too young and I miss her still
But she stays within me and always will

A Farewell To Arms

When Hemingway wrote A Farewell To Arms
It was a brilliant double metaphor
From what makes you stronger to that which harms
Referring to the end of love and war
For me it's limited to loss of love
Missing those arms and all they represent
That's the strongest image I can think of
An end to stimulation and content
It's been so long since they surrounded me
In a soft shell of strength and affection
And when hard times and strife confounded me
Their smooth bare beauty offered protection
It's so sad to lose the love and all its charms
Yet again I bid a farewell to arms

Silent Suffering

I suffer in silence but can't explain
Because no one would really understand
The breadth of my love the depth of my pain
And how things did not go as I had planned
Thoughts of you are keeping me up at night
My sensibility has been erased
I long for what seemed indelibly right
And all the pleasure on which it was based
The love you showed with your usual flair
Spreading so gradually outward in form
Whatever my troubles I did not care
Your laughter sheltered my mind from the storm
So yes I'll get by as I always do
Silently suffering days without you

Dylan Turns 80

Bob Dylan turned 80 the other day
Known as the voice of our generation
No one in music has had more to say
He's the William Shakespeare of this nation
His lyrics changed songwriting forever
From folk, R & B, blues, to rock 'n' roll
Deeply meaningful as well as clever
Intellectual but also with soul
He greatly inspires many of us
Writers poets and all music lovers
I'm quite sure you could get any of us
To quote a line from topics he covers
A true icon if I may be so bold
And now Bob Dylan is 80 years old

Waiting For the Sun

Sitting here waiting for the sun to shine
Metaphorically speaking I mean
I'm not at peace and that's the bottom line
Hoping best days are not already seen
That said maybe it's very natural
For people my age to see things this way
Because life evolving is actual
One can't expect the same as yesterday
If at times the sun goes behind a cloud
It doesn't mean the darkness has to fall
And if my spirits are under a shroud
It's not that the writing is on the wall
Though once again the shadows have begun
I sit patiently waiting for the sun

Sit and Be

We are addicted to activity
Keeping our minds busy every minute
Sometimes it's better to just sit and be
We don't have to join the race or win it
We're on our computer or on our phone
Every time there's a break in the action
We are terrified of feeling alone
Always needing the latest distraction
It's important to break this perceived need
For obsessive nonstop stimulation
Other parts of the psyche we must feed
Give that overworked mind a vacation
Sometimes our tired brains do need to rest
Just sitting and being might be the best

Duet Turns 2

A beautiful girl a glorious day
Bringing joy to everyone all the time
Every year at the very end of May
We celebrate this gentle child sublime
As I sit with my coffee this morning
Fresh-picked flowers offer their sweet perfume
Her beautiful image is adorning
The sun-filled corners of my springtime room
Her wide-eyed inquisitive cherub face
Takes your mind off any troubles at hand
Makes it so much easier to erase
Those feelings of doubt that will take command
As warm sun dries the early morning dew
Our most precious Duet is turning 2

The Doors of Ecstasy

You graciously laid out the welcome mat
As I approached the doors of ecstasy
I hoped and prayed that I had arrived at
The warm home of my lifelong fantasy
As I apprehensively rang the bell
I really didn't know what to expect
Would the tall doors of ecstasy foretell
An opening of comfort and respect
For a while it was pure heaven on earth
I was as happy as a man could be
I tried to give you all that I was worth
To keep open the doors of ecstasy
It wasn't enough and you had to flee
So I left closing those doors behind me

Listen To Music

Listen to music when you're feeling low
I guarantee it will improve your mood
Whether it's current or from long ago
It brings joy and leaves your spirits renewed
Alternative hip-hop or rock 'n' roll
Classical country R&B or jazz
Food for the mind and comfort for the soul
It's kept me going like nothing else has
Try to listen without a distraction
Giving the music your full attention
I guarantee you'll have a reaction
It's a feeling beyond comprehension
If you're feeling down and troubled, who knows
Listening to music could cure your woes

She Walks With the Angels

———◆———

She walks with the angels as it should be
Because they're in need of a protégé
As endearing as a person could be
A calm to the night a warmth to the day
The angels gave her a heart of pure gold
With a mind that flows like a waterfall
Kind and intelligent humble and bold
Her generosity is there for all
She walks with the angels from coast to coast
While bearing gifts at full capacity
Without pretension or even a boast
Just dedication and vivacity
Although it's true she flies with her own wings
She walks with the angels as love she brings

The Quiet

---·•·---

I sit and try to embrace the quiet
It rings in my ears and plays with my mind
For some reason I try to deny it
Cuz the tranquility appears unkind
This is a paradox I've often faced
An irrational need for commotion
While I know that desire is misplaced
It seems to be a stubborn emotion
In many respects I've always longed for
Peace and quiet while being reflective
And in the past I've often been wronged for
Forging ahead and losing perspective
Though it seems daunting I think I'll try it
Being still and embracing the quiet

The Sound of My Words

This is a tribute to my dear friend Gene
Who lends his voice to my written sonnet
From intensity to sweetly serene
Laying layers of pure love upon it
Jerry to my Hunter - that melody
Fills the air with precise intonation
Playing with structure bringing clarity
Always with mindful consideration
These readings are not easy to come by
It takes years of patient dedication
Precious few can do it though many try
To perfect this soulful recitation
He truly understands what my words mean
Thus I offer my gratitude to Gene

THE END

Made in the USA
Las Vegas, NV
31 October 2021

33455430R00065